How I Feel: Grief Journal for Kids

HOW I FEEL

GRIEF JOURNAL FOR KIDS

Guided Prompts to Explore Your Feelings and Find Peace

MIA ROLDAN, LCSW, LCDC

ROCKRIDGE
PRESS

I dedicate this book to all children who have lost something or someone special. Your sadness is real, and your pain matters.

Interior and Cover Designer: Stephanie Sumulong
Art Producer: Alyssa Williams
Editor: Barbara J. Isenberg
Production Editor: Matthew Burnett
Production Manager: Martin Worthington

All Illustrations © olga.angelloz/Creative Market
Author photograph courtesy of Ryan Andrews / @photographeelings

Paperback ISBN: 978-1-63807-879-1
R0

This Journal Belongs To

_____

IN MEMORY OF

CONTENTS

INTRODUCTION

Welcome to your own personal grief journal. My name is Mia, and I will be your guide throughout this book. I am a teacher and a therapist, and I have two sons. I also know what it's like to experience a difficult loss. I understand how hard it is to lose someone or something super important to you. In this book, I'm going to help you explore your feelings about your loss. Someone who cares a lot about you gave this book to you, and I am glad they did. It is so important to have people in our lives who love us and take care of us.

Right now, you are probably feeling a lot of different emotions. You might be confused, sad, scared, overwhelmed—maybe all these things at once! These feelings are okay and totally normal. This book is a private and safe place just for you to write down anything you are feeling about your loss.

You can write or draw as little or as much as you want in this book. Some days you may have a lot to share. Other days your feelings might be too difficult to think about. That's okay. You can go through this book at your own pace—every day, every week, or whenever it feels right for you. It's also a special kind of book because you don't have to start at the beginning. You can skip around and write from any place. You have as much freedom as you want when it comes to writing about *your* feelings.

As soon as you're ready, let's get started.

PART ONE

Explore Your Feelings

There's a lot going on inside of you right now. On most days you probably feel a range of different emotions. You may be happy, curious, or surprised. Some days you may even feel a little sad or angry. But when you lose someone or something important, there are many more thoughts and feelings that you will have. And they may feel so much stronger. Some feelings may make sense, but others can be confusing for your mind and your body. This is normal and something that happens to everyone. In this book you'll learn about these new feelings inside of you and how you can better understand what's going on.

BEING GRATEFUL

Some families, at dinnertime or on holidays, like to go around the table and have everyone say who or what they are grateful for. When you lose someone or something important, it can be helpful to remember all the special people and things you have in your life. Write down everything you are grateful for here.

_____

_____

_____

_____

_____

_____

_____

_____

_____

_____

_____

_____

YOUR HAPPY LIST

We all have things in our life that make us happy. Maybe it's a pet, a special place you have been, or a favorite activity. When you experience a loss, it helps to have a reminder of all these things in one place. Make a list of everything that makes you happy.

YOUR HEALING PLACE

Having a special place to go where you feel safe and relaxed is helpful when you're feeling a lot of emotions.

1. Select your own special place. Maybe it's a cozy corner of a room in your house or your favorite spot at a park.

2. Gather some of your favorite things to make your space as comfortable as possible.

3. Let your family know that this is your own private place.

How do you feel when you're in your healing place?

_____

_____

_____

_____

_____

_____

_____

_____

_____

_____

YOUR SUPERPOWER

Imagine you are a superhero with a really cool super-power. What would your superpower be? Draw yourself as a superhero in the box below.

UNIQUE YOU

What are some things that you're good at doing? Is there anything really interesting or special about you? Share some of the things that make you unique here.

_____

_____

_____

_____

_____

_____

_____

_____

_____

_____

_____

_____

_____

_____

_____

_____

YOUR PEOPLE

Think about all the people you know—your family, teachers, neighbors, and friends. Who are the people in your life that you can talk to about anything? Write down their names here.

_____

_____

_____

_____

_____

_____

_____

_____

_____

_____

_____

_____

_____

_____

SADNESS

When you're sad, it can change your energy level and make even the simplest tasks seem difficult. When was the last time you felt sad?

_____

_____

_____

_____

_____

_____

_____

What made you sad? What did your sadness feel like?

_____

_____

_____

_____

_____

_____

_____

Was there someone who was helpful when you were sad? What did that person do to help you feel better?

_____

_____

_____

_____

_____

_____

_____

_____

_____

_____

_____

_____

_____

_____

_____

LET IT GO

Feelings have a way of building up inside us. Here's a way to let go of some of those difficult feelings.

1. Go outside with a bottle of bubbles.

2. Before blowing bubbles, take a deep breath and hold it for three seconds. Think about all the emotions you're feeling right now.

3. As you exhale through the wand, release your feelings and imagine them inside the bubbles. As the bubbles float away, imagine your feelings drifting away, too. When the bubbles pop, imagine your feelings disappearing.

How did this exercise make you feel?

_____

_____

_____

_____

_____

_____

_____

_____

_____

OUR MASK

Sometimes you may tell people you're feeling one way, but on the inside there are a lot of other things going on that you don't want to share. It's like you're wearing a mask and people can't see what's really going on inside you. In the first box below, draw a picture of your face wearing the mask you choose to show people. Then in the other box, draw a picture of your face without your mask. Show the feelings that you keep inside and don't let people see.

DRAW

DRAW

CHANGE

Write down all the things that have changed in your life since your loss.

_____

_____

_____

_____

_____

_____

_____

_____

_____

_____

_____

_____

_____

_____

WHAT IS DIFFERENT?

What change has been the hardest? Why?

_____

_____

_____

_____

_____

_____

_____

_____

_____

_____

_____

_____

_____

_____

_____

_____

WHAT IS YOUR ANGER LIKE?

Unexpected change can be hard to accept. It can bring a lot of strong feelings, too—even anger. What feelings do you have about how things have changed?

_____

_____

_____

_____

_____

_____

_____

What does anger feel like in your body?

_____

_____

_____

_____

_____

_____

What are some things you do that help you when you feel angry?

_____

_____

_____

_____

_____

_____

_____

_____

_____

_____

_____

_____

_____

_____

_____

_____

TEAR IT UP!

This is a good activity to do when you feel angry.

1. Go to your healing place with a piece of paper and a pencil or pen.

2. Write down everything that's making you angry right now. Don't hold anything back!

3. When you're finished, tear up the paper. Keep tearing it into the smallest pieces that you can.

What did it feel like to tear up your anger?

_____

_____

_____

_____

_____

_____

_____

_____

_____

_____

_____

YOUR ANGER

Your anger can be overwhelming, and it can sometimes feel like it controls you. Draw a picture of what you think your anger looks like. Then give your anger a name. This will help you recognize that the anger you feel is separate from who you are.

RULES AND RESPONSIBILITIES

What are some rules your parents or caregivers give you to follow? How do these rules make you feel?

_____

_____

_____

_____

_____

_____

_____

_____

_____

_____

_____

_____

_____

_____

_____

_____

ROUTINES

Having a consistent routine can help you feel calm because you know there are things you can count on. What is your daily routine? How does having a routine make you feel? What would you change about your daily routine right now if you could?

_____

_____

_____

_____

_____

_____

_____

_____

_____

_____

_____

_____

_____

_____

_____

FAVORITE ACTIVITIES

What are your favorite activities to do with your family or friends?

_____

_____

_____

_____

_____

_____

_____

What is something that you used to enjoy, but since your loss, you don't feel like doing anymore?

_____

_____

_____

_____

_____

_____

What new activity would you like to try?

_____

_____

_____

_____

_____

_____

_____

_____

_____

_____

_____

_____

_____

_____

_____

_____

_____

_____

YOUR CALM SPACE

Everyone has a place that makes them feel calm and peaceful. Sometimes it's a real place you've been to. Sometimes you've only gone there in your imagination. What place makes you feel at peace? Draw a picture of it here.

DRAW

MAKE A CALMING JAR

You can make a calming jar at home with just a few items.

1. Find a medium or large jar with a top. Make sure it is clean inside.

2. Fill the jar with warm water.

3. Add glitter paint or glitter glue.

4. Add any kind of small objects you like—small toys, shells, charms, buttons, etc.

5. Make sure the top is on tight, then shake up the jar and watch the glitter and objects slowly settle to the bottom.

How do you feel as you watch the items in your calming jar? Does this help you feel relaxed?

_____

_____

_____

_____

_____

_____

_____

_____

TALK ABOUT YOU

How would you describe yourself to someone who has never met you? Write about yourself here.

_____

_____

_____

_____

_____

_____

_____

_____

_____

_____

_____

_____

_____

_____

FEAR

Write about a time when you were afraid to try something new. What did you do to conquer your fear? How did you feel afterward?

_____

_____

_____

_____

_____

_____

_____

_____

_____

_____

_____

_____

_____

_____

_____

_____

_____

CONFIDENCE

What does confidence mean to you? Describe the ways
that you feel you are a confident person.

_____

_____

_____

_____

_____

_____

_____

_____

_____

_____

_____

_____

_____

_____

_____

ROLE MODEL

A role model is a person you look up to and admire. Name a role model in your life. What is it about them that inspires you?

_____

_____

_____

_____

_____

_____

_____

_____

_____

_____

_____

_____

_____

_____

_____

PART TWO

Create Comfort

We all have things that make us feel better when we're sick, worried, afraid, or experiencing a difficult situation. Some helpful activities might be talking to a friend, drawing, or being with your pet. You might have other things that help you, too. Think of these as your special tools that work just for you. In this section of your journal, you're going to put all your tools in one place, sort of like a toolbox. When you're sad from a loss of someone or something important to you, it's helpful to have your toolbox ready with ideas you can use at any time.

FUN!

If I asked you what's the most fun you've ever had, what would you say? Think about trips, parties, vacations, holidays, or any other time when you had fun. Write about those experiences here.

_____

_____

_____

_____

_____

_____

_____

_____

_____

_____

_____

_____

_____

_____

_____

_____

COMFORT OBJECT

Do you have an object that is so special to you that just seeing it and holding it can make you feel better? Write about your comfort object here.

_____

_____

_____

_____

_____

_____

_____

_____

_____

_____

_____

_____

_____

_____

_____

_____

_____

LAUGH-A-DAY CLUB

Laughing makes your whole body and mind feel better. When you laugh, it also makes other people feel good, too.

1. Start a club at your house called the Laugh-a-Day Club. Make a sign for your club and decorate it.

2. Invite your family members to join the club. Explain that everyone will take turns making each other laugh by doing something funny, like telling a joke, doing a goofy dance, or sharing a silly story.

How do you feel when you're laughing with your family?

_____

_____

_____

_____

_____

_____

_____

_____

_____

CIRCLE OF CARE

In the smallest circle below, draw a picture of yourself. In the middle circle, write the names of your family members, pets, and friends. In the largest circle, write the names of five to ten people from your school, neighborhood, and community. This picture is a reminder that you're always surrounded by love and care.

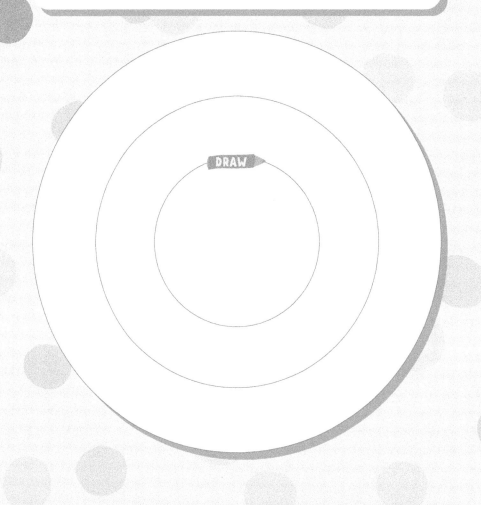

DRAW

KEEPING BUSY

Having distractions can really help when you're having a bad day. What are some things you like to do to keep busy? Some ideas might be working on a puzzle, drawing, or putting together a model. Write down different ways that you like to keep busy.

_____

_____

_____

_____

_____

_____

_____

_____

_____

_____

_____

_____

_____

_____

WHAT WOULD YOUR BEST FRIEND SAY?

Sometimes it's easier to say kind words to other people than to ourselves. Practice your own kind words here by writing down what you would tell your best friend if they had a big loss in their life. What would you say to comfort and support them?

YOUR PERFECT DAY

If you could create a perfect day to spend any way you wanted, what would that day look like?

_____

_____

_____

_____

Who would you spend the day with, and why?

_____

_____

_____

_____

_____

What things would you do?

_____

_____

_____

_____

_____

Circle the things you wrote that you can actually do right now. How will doing these activities make you feel?

_____

_____

_____

_____

_____

_____

_____

_____

_____

_____

_____

_____

_____

_____

_____

_____

_____

_____

_____

MAGIC MACHINE

This is an activity you can do by yourself or with your family and friends.

1. Get a blanket or a sheet and lots of pillows.

2. Spread your blanket or sheet somewhere in your backyard or on your living room floor. Arrange your pillows like comfortable chairs or seats. Bring some snacks, too.

3. Pretend you're riding in a magic machine that can fly you anywhere in the world.

Where would you decide to go? What kinds of things would you see there? What activities would you do?

_____

_____

_____

_____

_____

_____

_____

_____

_____

COMFORT BOARD

Create a picture collage of all the things that make you happy. Cut out pictures from magazines, print photos from online sites, or draw your own images. Glue or tape these items on this page.

DRAW

LEARNING FROM YOUR PAST

Think of a challenging time in your life. What sort of emotions did you feel? Who helped you during that time? What did you learn about yourself from that experience?

_____

_____

_____

_____

_____

_____

_____

_____

_____

_____

_____

_____

_____

_____

_____

AWESOME YOU!

What are three things about yourself that you love, and why?

_____

_____

_____

_____

_____

_____

_____

_____

_____

_____

_____

_____

_____

_____

_____

_____

ENCOURAGEMENT

Encouragement can help you feel stronger when you're coping with something difficult. How do your parents or caregivers encourage you?

_____

_____

_____

_____

_____

_____

How do people at school—your teachers, counselors, or coaches—encourage you? Do your friends encourage you, too?

_____

_____

_____

_____

_____

_____

_____

What does it feel like when people encourage you? How does it affect your confidence?

_____

_____

_____

_____

_____

_____

_____

_____

_____

_____

_____

_____

_____

_____

_____

_____

YOUR SLEEP

Getting regular sleep is important for your focus, health, and overall mood. Our bodies and minds depend on sleep to recharge and refill our energy tanks each day. Have you ever had trouble going to sleep or staying asleep? If so, try these suggestions to see if they help.

1. Go to bed and wake up at the same time every day.

2. Before bedtime, take a calm, warm bath to help you feel sleepy.

3. Put away all electronic devices with screens two hours before your bedtime. Spend time before bed reading, listening to music, drawing, or talking with your family.

Try these tips for five days in a row. Did they help? How did you feel at the end of the five days?

_____

_____

_____

_____

_____

_____

_____

AT PEACE

Think of a time when you felt completely relaxed and at peace—a time when you had no worries at all. Draw a picture of that memory.

MAGIC WAND

Imagine you have a magic wand. What would you do
with it?

_____

_____

_____

_____

_____

_____

_____

_____

_____

_____

_____

_____

_____

_____

THE REAL YOU

What is something that most people don't know about you? Is there something people think about you that you feel isn't true?

_____

_____

_____

_____

_____

_____

_____

_____

_____

_____

_____

_____

_____

_____

_____

_____

_____

FAMILY TRADITIONS

What are your favorite family traditions?

_____

_____

_____

_____

_____

_____

_____

What parts of these traditions do you enjoy the most?

_____

_____

_____

_____

_____

_____

_____

How does having family traditions to look forward to make you feel?

_____

_____

_____

_____

_____

_____

_____

_____

_____

_____

_____

_____

_____

_____

THE PRETZEL

This is a good exercise to do when you're feeling a lot of difficult emotions.

1. Clear a space on the floor where you can sit comfortably.

2. Sit with your legs crossed. Lift your knees up, then wrap your arms around them like a pretzel.

3. In this pretzel position, give yourself a big hug or squeeze. Hold this pose and count to five, then release.

4. Using a timer or with a clock nearby, repeat this exercise for five more minutes.

How did you feel during this exercise? How did you feel when you were done?

_____

_____

_____

_____

_____

_____

_____

YOUR SADNESS

Draw a picture of what your sadness looks and feels like to you.

NATURE

Nature has a powerful effect on us. Just being by the ocean or hiking in the woods can help us feel better. If you could experience any type of nature right now, what would you choose and why?

_____

_____

_____

_____

_____

_____

_____

_____

_____

_____

_____

_____

_____

_____

_____

MAKE A SUGGESTION

Pretend there's a suggestion box on your kitchen table. What suggestion would you put in the box that would make you feel better right now?

FAVORITES

A good story can lift our mood and help us forget our troubles for a while. What is your favorite story of all time? It can be from a movie or a book. What does the story mean to you?

_____

_____

_____

_____

_____

_____

_____

_____

_____

_____

_____

_____

_____

_____

_____

LOVE

What makes you feel most loved? What actions and words from people let you know that you're loved?

_____

_____

_____

_____

_____

_____

_____

_____

_____

_____

_____

_____

_____

_____

_____

_____

_____

_____

PART THREE

Find Peace

Losing someone or something important to you is an experience that will change with time. Some days it feels painful, other days you feel comfort from your memories, and then there will be days when you don't think about it at all. All of this is okay! Stay curious about your feelings and continue to share them with the people who love you.

BEING STUCK

Sometimes painful feelings get stuck inside you and won't go away. You can let go of them here. First, identify the uncomfortable feelings you're having and write them down. Then practice getting rid of them by pretending you're throwing each one in a trash can.

_____

_____

_____

_____

_____

_____

_____

_____

_____

_____

_____

_____

_____

YOU ARE IN CONTROL

Some days it might feel like you are not in control of your behavior. But actually, you are *always* in control of everything you do. Think about one of the feelings you wrote about on the previous page. Using what you've learned, think about what *you* can do to make *yourself* feel better.

MEMORY CHAIN

Recall some memories of who or what you have lost. They can be memories of big events, like birthdays or holidays, or smaller moments, like a walk in a park. Make a memory chain of these special thoughts.

1. You will need some paper to write on, colored pencils or markers, tape or a stapler, and a pair of scissors.

2. Write down as many memories as you can think of. Then cut each one out. Each cut-out memory should be about the same size. Tape or staple your memories together to make a paper chain.

How do you feel seeing these memories all in one place?

_____

_____

_____

_____

_____

_____

_____

_____

FUTURE FIVE

Place your hand in the box and trace it. Inside each finger space, write something you're looking forward to or are excited about doing. It can be something coming up soon, or something far in the future.

POSITIVE SELF-TALK

Saying positive phrases to yourself is so important—especially when you're having a tough time with a big loss. Telling yourself encouraging words, as often as you can, will help you feel those things. Write down as many positive phrases you can think of on the following lines. Here are two to get started: "I am stronger than I know" and "I have people who love and care about me."

_____

_____

_____

_____

_____

_____

_____

_____

_____

_____

_____

_____

_____

WHAT WOULD YOU WANT TO SAY?

After the loss of someone special, there may be things you wanted to tell that person that you never got the chance to say. Or maybe there are things happening right now in your life that you would want to share. Use this space to tell your person something you really want them to know.

HOPE

Hope can help you stay positive, even when you're feeling down. Did you see or hear something this week that gave you hope? What was it?

_____

_____

_____

_____

_____

_____

_____

Why did it make you feel hopeful?

_____

_____

_____

_____

_____

_____

What does hope mean to you? Why do you think it's important to have hope?

REMEMBRANCE KEEPSAKE

Here is something you can create to tell the story of your loss.

1. Have an adult take you to a craft store to get beads and string to make a bracelet, necklace, or keychain.

2. Decide what each bead will represent. Some ideas are a special memory, a favorite food, a holiday, a pet, a trip, etc.

3. Thread the beads on the string. When all the beads are on, tie the two ends of the string together.

How does your keepsake connect you to what you have lost?

_____

_____

_____

_____

_____

_____

_____

FUTURE YOU

Draw a picture of how you see yourself in the future.

BEST FRIEND

Who is your best friend? How does your best friend make you feel?

_____

_____

_____

_____

_____

_____

_____

_____

_____

_____

_____

_____

_____

TRUST

Who do you trust the most in the world? What makes this person trustworthy?

_____

_____

_____

_____

_____

_____

_____

_____

_____

_____

_____

_____

_____

_____

_____

_____

_____

_____

BEING A HELPER

When was the last time you helped someone?

_____

_____

_____

_____

_____

_____

_____

How did being helpful make you feel?

_____

_____

_____

_____

_____

_____

_____

Do you feel comfortable asking for help? Why or why not?

WORRY BOX

Sometimes when you lose someone or something special, it might cause you to worry more than you usually do. And if you keep thinking about it, that worry can get bigger, until soon you're imagining the worst thing that could happen. Let's create a place to put all those worries and unhelpful thoughts.

1. Find a box with a lid. A shoebox will work just fine.

2. Decorate your box any way you'd like. Get creative with markers, glitter, ribbon, pictures . . . anything you'd like!

3. Whenever you have a worry that you can't get rid of, write it on a piece of paper and put the paper in your box.

4. When you're finished, put the worry box—and your worry—away. Keep the box somewhere where you can't see it, but you know that it's there.

How does it feel to let your worries go?

_____

_____

_____

_____

YOUR HEART

What feelings do you have inside you right now? Get some colored pencils or crayons. Draw lines in the heart below, to divide it into sections. Pick out colors to represent the different feelings you're having, then use those colors to fill in the sections of the heart. Each section is a different feeling.

MUSIC

Music can often help us express what we're feeling. What music do you like to listen to? How do you feel when you're listening to your favorite song or artist?

_____

_____

_____

_____

_____

_____

_____

_____

_____

_____

_____

_____

_____

_____

_____

_____

BEST TRIP EVER

What is the best trip you've ever been on? What made it so special?

_____

_____

_____

_____

_____

_____

_____

_____

_____

_____

_____

_____

_____

_____

_____

_____

_____

FAVORITE TEACHER

Who is your favorite teacher you've ever had?

_____

_____

_____

_____

_____

_____

_____

What is your favorite teacher like?

_____

_____

_____

_____

_____

_____

_____

What are some of the best things your teacher has taught you?

_____

_____

_____

_____

_____

_____

_____

_____

_____

_____

_____

_____

_____

_____

_____

_____

SUNSET

This is a good exercise to do with a friend or a family member.

1. Find out what time the sun goes down and invite a family member to join you to watch the sunset together.

2. Half an hour before sunset, get your favorite drinks and snacks together. Find a comfortable place to sit outside. You can also sit inside and watch the sunset through a window.

3. As you watch the sun go down, tell your family member about a feeling you have that is connected to your loss. Ask them to share how they're feeling, too.

How did you feel while watching the sunset? How did it feel to share your feelings?

_____

_____

_____

_____

_____

_____

_____

TREE OF STRENGTH

Trace your hand and wrist in the empty box. Be sure to leave your fingers open. This hand will be the trunk and the branches of your Tree of Strength. On each branch, write the name of someone you can talk to about your loss. Next, fill out the top of your tree with lots of leaves. Inside each leaf, write one thing that makes you happy.

DRAW

TRAVEL

If you could travel to three places with your family, where would you go? What do those places have in common? How are they different?

_____

_____

_____

_____

_____

_____

_____

_____

_____

_____

_____

_____

_____

_____

_____

YOUR GOAL

What is something you've always wanted to do? What things do you have to do to accomplish your goal?

RELIEF

Relief is what we feel when we no longer feel stressed or worried. Think of a time that you felt truly relieved. How did your body feel? What thoughts did you have?

_____

_____

_____

_____

_____

_____

_____

_____

_____

_____

_____

_____

_____

_____

_____

REMEMBER TO LOOK AROUND YOU

Books and movies with heroes or strong main characters often show something difficult that happened to them in their past. But with support and guidance, they were able to feel happiness and find joy again. Think about some of your favorite heroes and characters and how they overcame their difficulties. Now that you've come to the end of this book, where do you find support and guidance in your life?

RESOURCES

WEBSITES

The Christi Center, Austin TX: ChristiCenter.org
The Christi Center is a grief and loss agency that serves any child, teen, or adult who is grieving the death of a loved one. They offer all services free of charge.

The Dougy Center, Portland, OR: Dougy.org
The Dougy Center has developed a wide range of resources for children, teens, young adults, and families who are grieving, supporters of people who are grieving, and counselors and helping professionals.

The National Alliance for Children's Grief: ChildrenGrieve.org
The National Alliance for Children's Grief (NACG) is a nonprofit organization that raises awareness about the needs of children and teens who are grieving a death and provides education and resources for anyone who supports them.

Helping Kids Grieve with Sesame Street: SesameStreetInCommunities .org/topics/grief
Articles, videos, activities, and other resources about grief and loss for children and families.

Mindfulness & Grief Institute: MindfulnessAndGrief.com
Mindfulness-based grief support that tends to your body, spirit, and mind.

New York Life Foundation: NewYorkLife.com/foundation
The New York Life Foundation strives to support young people, particularly in the areas of educational enhancement and childhood bereavement support.

Psychology Today: PsychologyToday.com/us
Psychology Today has a comprehensive list of therapists within the US. You can search by location, specialties, age, insurance, and modalities.

ARTICLES

"Understanding Grief," by Jane E. Brody, *The New York Times*. NYTimes.com/2018/01/15/well/live/understanding-grief.html

"Grief: Recommendations for Helping Students Who Have Experienced a Significant Loss," University of Delaware. Education.UDel.edu/wp-content/uploads/2013/01/Grief.pdf.

"Helping Children Grieve: Tips for Parents," by Kathleen Smith, PsyCom. PsyCom.net/helping-children-grieve.

"When Children Grieve," by Edy Nathan, *Psychology Today*. PsychologyToday.com/us/blog/tales-grief/201903/when-children-grieve.

PODCASTS

"Helping Children Grieve" with Patrice Karst and hosted by Gabe Howard, *Inside Mental Health: A Psych Center Podcast*. PsychCentral.com/blog/podcast-helping-children-grieve#1.

"Stories for Death, Grief, and Loss," hosted by Silke Rose West and Joseph Sarosy, *How to Tell Stories to Children*. HowToTellStoriesToChildren.com/podcast-blog/stories-for-death-grief-and-loss.

"Children and Grief: How to Help Kids Cope with Loss Early in Life," with Jana DeCristofaro and hosted by Heather Stang, *Mindfulness and Grief Podcast*. MindfulnessAndGrief.com/children-and-grief-with-jana-decristofaro.

BOOKS

Healing Your Grieving Heart for Kids: 100 Practical Ideas, by Alan D. Wolfelt. The basic message of the book is that children need to mourn and express their grief outside themselves if they are to heal.

ABOUT THE AUTHOR

 **Mia Roldan,** LCSW, LCDC, is a licensed clinical social worker in Austin, Texas. Her first book, *Voices of Strength: Sons and Daughters of Suicide Speak Out*, coauthored with Judith Z. Fox, is about surviving a parent's suicide, which was Roldan's personal experience. Her second work, *Navigating Grief: A Guided Journal*, is a book for adults to reflect, cope, and heal from their grief. Grief and loss work is something Roldan has done her whole professional life, with adolescents, families, and adults in different educational and medical settings. She is a clinical social worker at the Adolescent Medicine Clinic with Dell Children's Medical Center. She works at the University of Texas at Austin's Dell Medical School's Department of Health Social Work and is a part of their Integrated Behavioral Health team. Additionally, Mia Roldan is an assistant professor of practice at the University of Texas at Austin's Steve Hicks School of Social Work. Find out more at MiaRoldanAustinTherapy.com.